I0423878

Born in 1988

By

Kerry Butters.

Born in 1988.

Millennium:	2nd millennium
Centuries:	19th century – **20th century** – 21st century
Decades:	1950s 1960s 1970s – **1980s** – 1990s 2000s 2010s
Years:	1985 1986 1987 – **1988** – 1989 1990 1991

1988 (MCMLXXXVIII) was a leap year starting on Friday (dominical letter CB) of the Gregorian calendar, the 1988th year of the Common Era (CE) and *Anno Domini* (AD) designations, the 988th year of the 2nd millennium, the 88th year of the 20th century, and the 9th year of the 1980s decade.

In the 20th century, the year **1988** has the most Roman numeral digits (11).

1988 was a crucial year in the early history of the Internet—it was the year of the first well-known computer virus, the 1988 Internet worm. The first permanent intercontinental Internet link was made between the United States (NSFNET) and Europe (Nordunet) as well as the first Internet-based chat protocol, Internet Relay Chat. The concept of the World Wide Web was first discussed at CERN in 1988.

The Soviet Union began its major restructuring towards a mixed economy at the beginning of 1988 and began its gradual collapse. The first extrasolar planet, Gamma Cephei Ab (confirmed in 2002) was detected this year and the World Health Organization began its mission to eradicate polio, a feat that is nearly complete as of 2015.

Contents

Events

January

- January – The cargo ship *Khian Sea* deposits 4,000 tons of toxic waste in Haiti after wandering around the Atlantic for sixteen months.
- January 1 – The Evangelical Lutheran Church in America is established, creating the largest Lutheran denomination in the United States.
- January 2
    - The Soviet Union begins its program of economic restructuring (perestroika) with legislation initiated by Premier Mikhail Gorbachev (though Gorbachev had begun minor restructuring in 1985).
    - Michigan State Spartans football team wins the Rose Bowl Game against USC Trojans.
- January 7–8 – In the Afghan War, 39 men of the Soviet Airborne Troops from the 345th Independent Guards Airborne Regiment fight off an attack by 200 to 250

Mujahideen in the Battle for Hill 3234, later dramatized in the Russian film *The 9th Company*

- January 13 – Taiwan President Chiang Ching-kuo dies in Taipei; Vice-President Lee Teng-hui becomes president.
- January 15 – In Jerusalem, Israeli police and Palestinian protestors clash at the Dome of the Rock; several police and at least 70 Palestinians are injured.
- January 17 – The long running Australian soap opera, *Home and Away* premieres on Seven Network.
- January 25 – U.S. Vice President George H. W. Bush and CBS News anchor Dan Rather clash over Bush's role in the Iran–Contra affair during a contentious television interview.
- January 26 – *The Phantom of the Opera*, the longest running Broadway play ever, opens.
- January 29 – The Midwest Classic Conference, a U.S. college athletic conference, is formed.

February

- February 3 – The Democratic-controlled United States House of Representatives rejects President Ronald Reagan's request for $36.25 million to support the Nicaraguan Contras.
- February 12
  - Anthony Kennedy is appointed to the Supreme Court of the United States.
  - The 1988 Black Sea bumping incident: Soviet frigate *Bezzavetnyy* intentionally rams USS *Yorktown* in Soviet territorial waters while *Yorktown* claims innocent passage.

- February 13 – 28 – The 1988 Winter Olympics are held in Calgary, Alberta, Canada.
- February 17
  - 1988 Oshakati bomb blast: A bomb explodes outside the First National Bank in Oshakati, Namibia, killing 27 and injuring 70.
  - U.S. Lieutenant Colonel William R. Higgins, serving with a United Nations group monitoring a truce in southern Lebanon, is kidnapped (and later killed by his captors).
- February 20 – The Nagorno-Karabakh Autonomous Oblast votes to secede from the Azerbaijan Soviet Socialist Republic and join the Armenian SSR, triggering the Nagorno-Karabakh War.
- February 24 – *Hustler Magazine v. Falwell*: The Supreme Court of the United States sides with *Hustler* magazine by overturning a lower court decision to award Jerry Falwell $200,000 for defamation.
- February 27 – February 29 – The Sumgait pogrom of Armenians occurs in Sumqayit.
- February 29 – A Nazi document implicates Kurt Waldheim in World War II deportations.

March

- March 3 – A new British political party, the Liberal Democrats, is formed.
- March 6 – Operation Flavius: A Special Air Service team of the British Army shoots dead 3 unarmed members of a

Provisional Irish Republican Army (IRA) Active service unit in Gibraltar.

- March 8
    - Two United States Army helicopters collide in Fort Campbell, Kentucky, killing 17 servicemen.
    - U.S. presidential candidate George H. W. Bush defeats Bob Dole in numerous Republican primaries and caucuses on "Super Tuesday". The bipartisan primary/caucus calendar, designed by Democrats to help solidify their own nominee early, backfires when none of the 6 competing candidates are able to break out of the pack in the day's Democratic contests. Jesse Jackson, however, wins several Southern state primaries.
- March 13
    - Opening to rail traffic of the Seikan Tunnel beneath the Tsugaru Strait connecting the Japanese islands of Honshu and Hokkaido (53.85 km (33.49 mi)), the world's longest (until 2016) and deepest.
    - Gallaudet University, a university for the deaf in Washington, D.C., elects Dr. I. King Jordan as the first deaf president in its history. This conclusion of the Deaf President Now campaign is a turning point in the deaf civil rights movement.
- March 16
    - The Halabja chemical attack is carried out by Iraqi government forces.
    - Iran–Contra affair: Lieutenant Colonel Oliver North and Vice Admiral John Poindexter are indicted on charges of conspiracy to defraud the United States.

- Milltown Cemetery attack: Three men are killed and 70 wounded in a gun and grenade attack by loyalist paramilitary Michael Stone on mourners at Milltown Cemetery in Belfast, Northern Ireland, during the funerals of the 3 IRA members killed in Gibraltar.
- First Republic Bank of Texas fails and enters FDIC receivership, the largest FDIC assisted bank failure in history.
- March 17
  - A Colombian Boeing 727 jetliner, Avianca Flight 410, crashes into the side of the mountains near the Venezuelan border, killing 143.
  - Eritrean War of Independence – Battle of Afabet: The Nadew Command, an Ethiopian army corps in Eritrea, is attacked on 3 sides by military units of the Eritrean People's Liberation Front (EPLF).
- March 19 – Corporals killings in Belfast: Two British Army corporals are abducted, beaten and shot dead by Irish republicans after driving into the funeral cortege of IRA members killed in the Milltown Cemetery attack.
- March 20 – Eritrean War of Independence: Having defeated the Nadew Command, the EPLF enters the town of Afabet, victoriously concluding the Battle of Afabet.
- March 24
  - An Israeli court sentences Mordechai Vanunu to 18 years in prison for disclosing Israel's nuclear program to *The Sunday Times*.
  - The first McDonald's restaurant in a country run by a Communist party opens in Belgrade, Yugoslavia. In

1989 it will be followed by one in Budapest, and in 1990 in Moscow and Shenzhen, China.

- March 25 – The Candle demonstration in Bratislava, Slovakia is the first mass demonstration of the 1980s against the socialist government in Czechoslovakia.
- March 26 – U.S. presidential candidate Jesse Jackson defeats Michael Dukakis in the Michigan Democratic caucuses, becoming the temporary front-runner for the party's nomination. Dick Gephardt withdraws his candidacy after his campaign speeches against imported automobiles fail to earn him much support in Detroit.
- March 29 – African National Congress representative Dulcie September is assassinated in Paris.

April

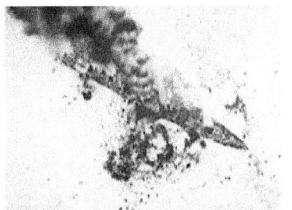

The Iranian Frigate, IS *Alvand*, attacked by US Navy forces during Operation Praying Mantis

- April 4 – Governor Evan Mecham of Arizona is convicted in his impeachment trial and removed from office.
- April 5
  - Massachusetts Governor Michael Dukakis wins the Wisconsin Democratic presidential primary.

- Kuwait Airways Flight 422 is hijacked while en route from Bangkok, Thailand to Kuwait. The hijackers demand the release of 17 Shiite Muslim prisoners held by Kuwait. Kuwait refuses to release the prisoners, leading to a 16-day siege across 3 continents. Two passengers are killed before the siege ends.
- April 10
  - Disneyland closes the America Sings Attraction permanently in Anaheim, California.
  - The comic strip *FoxTrot* makes its first appearance in US newspapers.
  - The Ojhri Camp Disaster occurs in Islamabad and Rawalpindi.
  - The Great Seto Bridge opens to traffic in Japan.
- April 11 – *The Last Emperor* (directed by Bernardo Bertolucci) wins nine Oscars.
- April 12 – Former pop singer Sonny Bono is elected mayor of Palm Springs, California.
- April 14
  - In the Geneva Accords, the Soviet Union commits itself to withdrawal of its forces from Afghanistan.
  - The USS *Samuel B. Roberts* (FFG-58) strikes a naval mine in the Persian Gulf, while deployed on Operation Earnest Will, during the Tanker War phase of the Iran–Iraq War.
- April 16
  - Israeli commandos kill the PLO's Abu Jihad in Tunisia.
  - In Forlì, Italy, the Red Brigades kill Senator Roberto Ruffilli, an advisor of Prime Minister Ciriaco De Mita.

- April 18 – The United States Navy retaliates for the USS *Samuel B. Roberts* mining with Operation Praying Mantis, in a day of strikes against Iranian oil platforms and naval vessels.
- April 20 – The world's longest skyjacking comes to an end when the remaining passengers of Kuwait Airways Flight 422 are released by their captors.
- April 22 – The Ouvéa cave hostage taking begins in Ouvéa, Loyalty Islands, New Caledonia.
- April 25 – In Israel, Ivan Demjanjuk is sentenced to death for war crimes committed in World War II. He is accused by survivors of being the notorious guard at the Treblinka extermination camp known as "Ivan the Terrible". The conviction is later overturned by the Israeli Supreme Court.
- April 28 – Aloha Airlines Flight 243 loses several yards of its upper fuselage while in flight, killing 1 person.
- April 29 – Boeing 747-400's first flight
- April 30
  - World Expo 88 opens in Brisbane Queensland, Australia.
  - Celine Dion wins the Eurovision Song Contest for Switzerland with the song "Ne partez pas sans moi".

May

- May 4 – PEPCON disaster in Henderson, Nevada: A major explosion at an industrial solid-fuel rocket plant causes damage extending up to 10 miles (16 km) away, including Las Vegas' McCarran International Airport.

- May 5 – The Ouvéa cave hostage taking ends in Ouvéa, Loyalty Islands, New Caledonia.
- May 14 – Bus collision near Carrollton, Kentucky: A drunk driver going the wrong way on Interstate 71, hits a converted school bus carrying a church youth group from Radcliff, Kentucky. The resulting fire kills 27, making it tied for 1st in the U.S. for most fatalities involving 2 vehicles to the present day. Coincidentally, the other 2-vehicle accident involving a bus that also killed 27 occurred in Prestonburg, Kentucky on February 28, 1958.
- May 15 – Soviet war in Afghanistan: After more than 8 years of fighting, the Soviet Army begins withdrawing from Afghanistan.
- May 16
    - A report by U.S. Surgeon General C. Everett Koop states that the addictive properties of nicotine are similar to those of heroin and cocaine.
    - *California v. Greenwood*: The U.S. Supreme Court rules that police officers do not need a search warrant to search through discarded garbage.
- May 24 – Section 28 (outlawing promotion of homosexuality in schools) is passed as law by Parliament in the United Kingdom.
- May 27 – Microsoft releases Windows 2.1.
- May 31 – U.S. President Ronald Reagan addresses 600 Moscow State University students, during his visit to the Soviet Union.

June

- June – US congress approved expansion of Medicare benefits to protect against "catastrophic" medical costs; the act was repealed in November 1989.
- June 5 – The first National Cancer Survivors Day is held.
- June 6 – Elizabeth II strips jockey Lester Piggott of his OBE, following his jailing for tax irregularities.
- June 10–14 – Spontaneous 100,000 strong mass night-singing demonstrations in Estonian SSR eventually give name to the Singing Revolution.
- June 11
  - The name of the General Public License (GPL) is mentioned for the first time.
  - Wembley Stadium hosts a concert featuring stars from the fields of music, comedy and film, in celebration of the 70th birthday of imprisoned ANC leader Nelson Mandela.
- June 14 – A small wildfire starts in Montana just north of the boundary for Yellowstone National Park. The Storm Creek fire expands into the park, then merges with dozens of other drought-inspired fires. Eventually, over 750,000 acres (3,000 km²) of Yellowstone – 36% of the park's area – burns before firefighters gain control in late September.
- June 23 – NASA scientist James Hansen testifies to the Senate that man-made global warming has begun.
- June 25 – The Netherlands defeats the Soviet Union 2–0 to win Euro 88.

- June 26 – Air France Flight 296 crashes into the tops of trees beyond the runway on a demonstration flight at Habsheim, France; 3 passengers are killed.
- June 27 – The Gare de Lyon rail accident occurs in Paris, France as a commuter train headed inbound to the terminal crashes into a stationary outbound train, killing 56 and injuring 57.
- June 28 – Four workers are exposed to poisonous gas at a metal-plating plant in Auburn, Indiana, in the worst confined-space industrial accident in U.S. history (a fifth victim dies two days later).
- June 29 – *Morrison v. Olson*: The United States Supreme Court upholds the law allowing special prosecutors to investigate suspected crimes by executive branch officials.
- June 30 – Roman Catholic Archbishop Marcel Lefebvre consecrates four bishops at Écône, Switzerland for his apostolate, along with Bishop Antonio de Castro Mayer, without a papal mandate.

July

- July 1 – The Soviet Union votes to end the CPSU's monopoly on economic and other non-political power and to further economic changes towards a less rigidly Marxist-Leninist economy.
- July 3
  - The Fatih Sultan Mehmet Bridge in Istanbul, Turkey is completed, providing the second connection between the continents of Europe and Asia over the Bosphorus.

- Iran Air Flight 655 is accidentally shot down by a missile launched from the USS *Vincennes*.
- July 6
    - The Piper Alpha production platform in the North Sea is destroyed by explosions and fires, killing 165 oil workers and 2 rescue mariners. 61 workers survive.
    - The first reported medical waste on beaches in the Greater New York area (including hypodermic needles and syringes possibly infected with the AIDS virus) washes ashore on Long Island. Subsequent medical waste discoveries on beaches in Coney Island, Brooklyn and in Monmouth County, New Jersey force the closure of numerous New York–area beaches in the middle of one of the hottest summers on record in the American Northeast.
- July 14 – Volkswagen closes its Westmoreland Assembly Plant after 10 years of operation (the first factory built by a non-American automaker in the U.S.).
- July 16 – Paddy Ashdown becomes the leader of the Liberal Democrats in the UK.
- July 20 – The Democratic National Convention in Atlanta nominates Michael Dukakis and Lloyd Bentsen as its Presidential and Vice Presidential candidates.
- July 31 – Thirty-two people are killed and 1,674 injured when a bridge at the Sultan Abdul Halim Ferry terminal collapses in Butterworth, Malaysia.

August

- August 5
    - Arif Hussain Hussaini, leader of Pakistani Shia Muslims, is shot in Peshawar.
    - The 1988 Malaysian constitutional crisis culminates in the ouster of the Lord President of Malaysia, Salleh Abas.
- August 6 – 7 – Tompkins Square Park Police Riot in New York City: A riot erupts in Tompkins Square Park when police attempt to enforce a newly passed curfew for the park. Bystanders, artists, residents, homeless people and political activists are caught up in the police action that takes place during the night of August 6 and early into August 7.
- August 8 – 8888 Uprising: Thousands of protesters in Burma, now known as *Myanmar*, are killed during anti-government demonstrations.
- August 11 – Al-Qaeda is formed by Osama bin Laden.
- August 14 – Enzo Ferrari, founder of the Italian automobile manufacturer Ferrari, dies at the age of 90, after a long illness.
- August 17 – Pakistani President Muhammad Zia-ul-Haq and the U.S. ambassador to Pakistan, Arnold Lewis Raphel, are killed in a plane crash near Bahawalpur.
- August 18 – The Republican National Convention in New Orleans, Louisiana nominates George H. W. Bush for President and Dan Quayle for Vice President of the United States of America.
- August 19 – A truce begins in the Iran–Iraq War.

- August 20 – The Iran–Iraq War ends, with an estimated one million lives lost.
- August 21 – The 6.9 Mw Nepal earthquake shakes the Nepal–India border with a maximum Mercalli intensity of VIII (*Severe*), leaving 709–1,450 people killed and thousands injured.
- August 25 – A fire destroys part of Chiado quarter, in Lisbon's historical center.
- August 26 – Mehran Karimi Nasseri, "The terminal man", decides to stay at the De Gaulle Airport in Paris, where he will continue to reside until August 1, 2006.
- August 28 – Seventy-five people are killed and 346 injured in one of the worst air show disasters in history at Germany's Ramstein Air Base, when three jets from the Italian air demonstration team, *Frecce Tricolori*, collide, sending one of the aircraft crashing into the crowd of spectators.

September

- September 5 – With US$2 billion in federal aid, the Robert M. Bass Group agrees to buy the United States' largest thrift, American Savings and Loan Association.
- September 11 – In Estonian SSR, 300,000 demonstrate for independence.
- September 12 – Hurricane Gilbert devastates Jamaica; it turns towards Mexico's Yucatán Peninsula 2 days later, causing an estimated $5 billion in damage.
- September 16 – Tom Browning of the Cincinnati Reds pitches the 12th perfect game in baseball history against the Los Angeles Dodgers at Riverfront Stadium.

- September 17 – October 2 – The 1988 Summer Olympics are held in Seoul, South Korea.
- September 22 – The Ocean Odyssey drilling rig suffers a blowout and fire in the North Sea (see also July 6).
- September 24 – 26 – Large, militant protests against the 1988 World Bank and IMF meetings take place in West Berlin.
- September 29 – *STS-26*: NASA resumes Space Shuttle flights, grounded after the *Challenger* disaster, with Space Shuttle *Discovery*.

October

- October 5
  - Thousands riot in Algiers, Algeria against the National Liberation Front government; by October 10 the army has killed and tortured about 500 people in crushing the riots.
  - Chilean dictator Augusto Pinochet loses a national plebiscite on his rule; he relinquishes power in 1990.
  - In Omaha, Nebraska, in the only vice presidential debate of the 1988 U.S. presidential election, the Republican vice presidential nominee, Senator Dan Quayle of Indiana, insists he has as much experience in government as John F. Kennedy did when he sought the presidency in 1960. His Democratic opponent, Senator Lloyd Bentsen of Texas, replies, "Senator, I served with Jack Kennedy. I knew Jack Kennedy. Jack Kennedy was a friend of mine. Senator, you're no Jack Kennedy."
- October 7 – *War of the Worlds* premieres in syndication.

- October 9 – The 1985–1988 Rugby League World Cup culminates in Australia's 25–12 victory over New Zealand at Auckland's Eden Park before 47,363 spectators.
- October 12
    - Walsh Street police shootings: Two Victoria Police officers are gunned down, execution style, in Australia.
    - The Birchandra Manu massacre occurs in Tripura, India.
- October 13 – In the second U.S. presidential debate, held by U.C.L.A., the Democratic party nominee, Michael Dukakis, is asked by journalist Bernard Shaw of CNN if he would support the death penalty if his wife, Kitty, were to be raped and murdered. Gov. Dukakis' reply, voicing his opposition to capital punishment in any and all circumstances, is later said to have been a major reason for the eventual failure of his campaign for the White House.
- October 15 – Kirk Gibson hits a dramatic home run to win Game 1 of the World Series for the Los Angeles Dodgers, over the Oakland Athletics, by a score of 5–4.
- October 19 – The United Kingdom bans broadcast interviews with IRA members. The BBC gets around this stricture through the use of professional actors.
- October 27 – Ronald Reagan decides to tear down the new U.S. Embassy in Moscow because of Soviet listening devices in the building structure.
- October 28 – Abortion: 48 hours after announcing it was abandoning RU-486, French manufacturer Roussel Uclaf states that it will resume distribution of the drug.
- October 29 – Pakistan's General Rahimuddin Khan resigns from his post as the governor of Sindh, following attempts

by the President of Pakistan, Ghulam Ishaq Khan, to limit the vast powers Gen. Rahimuddin had accumulated.
- October 30
  - Ayrton Senna became Formula 1 champion for the first time by winning 1988 Japanese Grand Prix.
  - Philip Morris buys Kraft Foods for US$13.1 billion.
  - Expo '88 in Brisbane, Australia draws to a close.

November

- November 1 – In the Israeli election, Likud wins 47 seats, Labour wins 49, but Likud Prime Minister Yitzhak Shamir remains in office.
- November 2 – The Morris worm, the first computer worm distributed via the Internet, written by Robert Tappan Morris, is launched from Massachusetts Institute of Technology in the U.S.
- November 3 – 5 – Thousands of South Korean students demonstrate against former president Chun Doo-hwan.
- November 3 – Sri Lankan Tamil mercenaries try to overthrow the Maldivian government. At President Maumoon Abdul Gayoom's request, the Indian military suppresses the coup attempt within 24 hours.
- November 8 – United States presidential election, 1988: George H. W. Bush is elected over Michael Dukakis, becoming the first sitting Vice President of the United States in 152 years to be elected as President of the United States.
- November 10 – The United States Air Force acknowledges the existence of the Lockheed F-117 Nighthawk in a Pentagon press conference.

- November 11 – In Sacramento, California, police find a body buried in the lawn of 60-year-old boardinghouse landlady Dorothea Puente (7 bodies are eventually found and Puente is convicted of 3 murders and sentenced to life in prison).
- November 13 – Mulugeta Seraw, an Ethiopian law student in Portland, Oregon, is beaten to death by members of the Neo-Nazi group East Side White Pride.
- November 15
    - In the Soviet Union, the unmanned Shuttle *Buran* is launched by an Energia rocket on its maiden orbital spaceflight (the first and last space flight for the shuttle).
    - Israeli–Palestinian conflict: An independent State of Palestine is proclaimed at the Palestinian National Council meeting in Algiers, by a vote of 253–46.
    - The very first Fairtrade label, Max Havelaar, is launched by Nico Roozen, Frans van der Hoff and ecumenical development agency Solidaridad in the Netherlands.
- November 16
    - The Supreme Soviet of the Estonian SSR adopts the Estonian Sovereignty Declaration in which the laws of the Estonian SSR are declared supreme over those of the Soviet Union. The USSR declares it unconstitutional on 26 November. It is the first declaration of sovereignty from Moscow of any Soviet or Eastern Block entity.
    - In the first open election in more than a decade, voters in Pakistan choose populist candidate Benazir Bhutto to be Prime Minister. Elections are held as planned

despite head of state Zia-ul-Haq's death earlier in August.

- November 18 – War on Drugs: U.S. President Ronald Reagan signs a bill providing the death penalty for murderous drug traffickers.
- November 21
  - Canadian federal election, 1988: Brian Mulroney and the Progressive Conservative Party of Canada win a second majority government.
  - Ted Turner officially buys Jim Crockett Promotions, known as NWA Crockett, and turns it into World Championship Wrestling (WCW).
- November 22 – In Palmdale, California, the first prototype B-2 Spirit stealth bomber is revealed.
- November 23 – Former Korean president Chun Doo Hwan publicly apologizes for corruption during his presidency, announcing he will go into exile.
- November 24 – The popular American cult television comedy *Mystery Science Theater 3000* makes its debut on KTMA.
- November 30 – Kohlberg Kravis Roberts & Co. buys RJR Nabisco for US$25.07 billion in the biggest leveraged buyout deal of all time.

December

- December 1
  - Carlos Salinas de Gortari takes office as President of Mexico.
  - The first World AIDS Day is held.

- December 2
  - Benazir Bhutto is sworn in as Prime Minister of Pakistan, becoming the first woman to head the government of an Islam-dominated state.
  - A cyclone in Bangladesh leaves 5 million homeless and thousands dead.
- December 6
  - The Australian Capital Territory is granted self-government by the Australian Capital Territory (Self-Government) Act 1988.
  - Famous American vocalist Roy Orbison dies of a heart attack in Hendersonville, Tennessee aged 52.
- December 7
  - In Soviet Armenia, the Ms 6.8 Spitak earthquake kills nearly 25,000, injures 31,000 and leaves 400,000 homeless.
  - Estonian language replaces Russian as the official language of the Estonian SSR.
- December 9 – The last Dodge Aries and Plymouth Reliant roll off the assembly line in a Chrysler factory in the U.S.
- December 12 – The Clapham Junction rail crash in London kills 35 and injures 132.
- December 16 – Perennial U.S. presidential candidate Lyndon LaRouche is convicted of mail fraud.
- December 20 – The United Nations Convention Against Illicit Traffic in Narcotic Drugs and Psychotropic Substances is signed at Vienna.
- December 21

- Pan Am Flight 103 is blown up over Lockerbie, Scotland, killing a total of 270 people. Those responsible are believed to be Libyans.
  - Drexel Burnham Lambert agreed to plead guilty to insider trading and other violations and pay penalties of US$650 million.
- December 22 – Brazilian union and environmental activist Chico Mendes is assassinated.

Date unknown

- TAT-8, the first transatlantic telephone cable to use optical fibers, is completed. This led to more robust connections between the American and European Internet.
- Near the end of the year, the first proper and official Internet connection to Europe is made between Princeton, New Jersey and Stockholm, Sweden.
- Zebra mussels are found in the Great Lakes.
- Tim Berners-Lee begins to openly discuss his plans for what would become the World Wide Web at CERN.
- The U.S. Drought of 1988 causes big crop damage in many states, impacts many portions of the United States and causes around $60 billion in damage. Multiple regions suffer in the conditions. Heat waves cause 4,800 to 17,000 excess deaths while scorching many areas of the United States during 1988.
- The Russian Mafia begins to expand with the decay of the Soviet Union.

- The Communist Party of Britain is founded by a Marxist–Leninist faction of the Communist Party of Great Britain, after its leadership embraces Eurocommunism.

Births

January

Haley Bennett

Robert Sheehan

Skrillex

Ashton Eaton

Jade Ewen

- January 1 – Nelufar Hedayat, British television personality
- January 3
  - Jonny Evans, Northern Irish footballer
  - J. R. Hildebrand, American race car driver
- January 5
  - Luke Daniels, English footballer
  - Pauline, French composer, songwriter and singer
- January 7
  - Haley Bennett, American actress and singer
  - Hardwell, Dutch progressive and electro house DJ and music producer
  - Robert Sheehan, Irish actor
- January 8
  - Adrián López Álvarez, Spanish footballer
  - Allison Harvard, American model
  - Michael Mancienne, English footballer
- January 9
  - Marc Crosas, Spanish footballer
- January 12
  - Claude Giroux, Canadian ice hockey player
  - Andrew Lawrence, American actor
- January 14
  - Kacey Barnfield, English actress
  - Hakeem Nicks, American football player
  - Tom Rosenthal, English actor and comedian
- January 15
  - Jun. K, Korean vocalist (2PM)
  - Skrillex, American musician and DJ
  - Charlotte Sometimes, American singer/songwriter
- January 16 – Nicklas Bendtner, Danish footballer

- January 17 – Will Genia, Australian professional rugby union
- January 18
  - Ironik, British musician, DJ and rapper
  - Angelique Kerber, German tennis player
- January 19
  - JaVale McGee, American basketball player
  - Alexey Vorobyov (aka Alex Sparrow), Russian singer and actor
- January 20
  - Colin Bensadon, Gibraltarian swimmer
  - Benjamin Ulrich, German international rugby union player
- January 21
  - Ashton Eaton, American decathlete
  - Vanessa Hessler, American-Italian model and actress
- January 22
  - Greg Oden, American basketball player
  - Nick Palatas, American actor
- January 24 – Jade Ewen, English singer, songwriter, actress and former member of the Sugababes
- January 25 – Tatiana Golovin, French tennis player
- January 26
  - Gary Hooper, English footballer
  - Mia Rose, Portuguese and British singer-songwriter
- January 27
  - Alice Burdeu, Australian fashion model
  - Kerlon, Brazilian footballer
  - Liu Wen, Chinese model

- January 28 – Alexandra Krosney, American film and television actress
- January 29
  - Tatyana Chernova, Russian heptathlete
  - Stephanie Gilmore, Australian professional surfer

February

Ángel Di María

Maiara Walsh

Rihanna

- February 2 – Meghan Collison, Canadian model
- February 3
  - Cho Kyuhyun, Korean singer (Super Junior)
  - Gregory van der Wiel, Dutch international footballer
- February 4 – Carly Patterson, American gymnast
- February 6 – Bailey Hanks, American singer, actress and dancer
- February 5 – Karin Ontiveros, Mexican beauty queen
- February 7
  - Ai Kago, Japanese singer
  - Lee Joon, South Korean idol singer (MBLAQ), dancer, actor, model
  - Matthew Stafford, American football player
  - Taylor Mays, American football safety
- February 9 – Lotte Friis, Danish swimmer
- February 11 – Li Chun, Chinese singer
- February 12
  - Mike Posner, American singer, songwriter, and producer
  - Afshan Azad, English actress

- Greta Salpeter, American singer/songwriter, pianist (The Hush Sound, Gold Motel)
- February 13 – Aston Merrygold, English singer (JLS)
- February 14
  - Ángel Di María, Argentine footballer
  - Katie Boland, Canadian actress
  - Quentin Mosimann, Swiss singer
  - Olga Álava, Ecuadorian Miss Earth 2011 winner
- February 15
  - Denílson Pereira Neves, Brazilian footballer
  - Jessica De Gouw, Australian actress
- February 16 – Kim Soo-hyun, South Korean actor
- February 17
  - Natascha Kampusch, Austrian television hostess
  - Adil Rashid, English cricketer
- February 18
  - Mark Davies, English footballer
  - Maiara Walsh, Brazilian-American actress
  - The Blossom Twins, English twin professional wrestlers
  - Changmin, Korean singer, songwriter and occasional actor
- February 20
  - Rihanna, Barbadian pop singer
  - Jiah Khan, British Indian
  - Tracy Spiridakos, Canadian actress
- February 21 – Matthias de Zordo, German javelin thrower
- February 22
  - Ximena Navarrete, Miss Universe 2010
  - Efraín Juárez, Mexican footballer
  - Kevin Borlée, Belgian sprinter

- February 24 – Rodrigue Beaubois, French basketball player
- February 27 – Mitch Mustain, professional football and baseball player
- February 28 – Markéta Irglová, Czech songwriter
- February 29 – Lena Gercke, German fashion model

March

Gal Mekel

Stephen Curry

Sasha Grey

Jessie J

Ryan Kalish

- March 1 – Trevor Cahill, American baseball player
- March 2
  - James Arthur, British singer and musician
  - Vito Mannone, Italian footballer
  - Matthew Mitcham, Australian diver
  - Nadine Samonte, Filipina actress and commercial model
- March 3
  - Bella Heathcote, Australian actress
  - Michael Morrison, English footballer
  - Rafael Muñoz, Spanish swimmer
- March 4
  - Josh Bowman, English film and television actor
  - Gal Mekel, Israeli basketball player
- March 6
  - Agnes Carlsson, Swedish recording artist
  - Simon Mignolet, Belgian footballer
  - Lee Seung-hoon, South Korean speed skater
  - Elaine and Melanie Silver, American actresses
- March 8
  - Armanti Edwards, American football player
  - Johnny Ruffo, Australian singer-songwriter and dancer
- March 10 – Ivan Rakitić, Croatian and Swiss footballer
- March 11
  - Fábio Coentrão, Portuguese footballer
  - Katsuhiko Nakajima, Japanese professional wrestler
- March 12 – Elly Jackson, English singer-songwriter (La Roux)
- March 13 – Tiffany Two, World's oldest cat (d. 2015)
- March 14

- Stephen Curry, American professional basketball player
- Sasha Grey, American actress, model, author, musician, and former pornographic actress
- March 15 – James Reimer, Canadian professional ice hockey goaltender
- March 16 – Jhené Aiko, American singer-songwriter
- March 17 – Grimes, Canadian artist musician and music video director
- March 19 – Clayton Kershaw, American baseball player
- March 21 – Lee Cattermole, English footballer
- March 22 – Tania Raymonde, American actress
- March 24 – Finn Jones, English actor
- March 25
  - Big Sean, American rapper
  - Erik Knudsen, Canadian actor
  - Ryan Lewis, American musician
- March 26 – Suvi Koponen, Finnish fashion model
- March 27
  - Nazario Fiakaifonu, Vanuatuan judoka
  - Holliday Grainger, English screen and stage actress
  - Jessie J, English singer and songwriter
  - Brenda Song, American actress
  - Atsuto Uchida, Japanese footballer
- March 28
  - Ryan Kalish, American baseball player
  - Lacey Turner, English actress
- March 29 – Kelly Sweet, American singer
- March 30 – Richard Sherman, American football player

April

Haley Joel Osment

Sara Paxton

Juan Mata

- April 1
  - Alexander Bychkov, Russian serial killer

- o Brook Lopez, American basketball player
- o Ed Drewett, British singer
- April 2
  - o Jesse Plemons, American film and television actor
  - o Kimber James, American transsexual pornographic actor and escort
  - o Stephanie Cayo, Italian-Peruvian actress, singer and model
- April 3
  - o Kam Chancellor, American football player
  - o Brandon Graham, American football Linebacker
  - o Tim Krul, Dutch footballer
- April 5 – Daniela Luján, Mexican pop singer and actress
- April 6
  - o Fabrice Muamba, English footballer
  - o Mike Bailey, British actor
- April 7 – Ed Speleers, British actor
- April 8 – Saqib Saleem, Indian model and actor
- April 9 – Uee, South Korean idol singer and actress
- April 10 – Haley Joel Osment, American actor
- April 11
  - o Leland Irving, Canadian ice hockey player
  - o Pete Kozma, American baseball player
- April 12
  - o Jessie James, American country pop singer and songwriter
  - o Tone Damli, Norwegian singer
  - o April Rose Pengilly, Australian actor and former model
- April 13
  - o Anderson Luís de Abreu Oliveira, Brazilian footballer

- o Allison Williams, American actress
- April 14 – Ben Lloyd-Hughes, British actor
- April 15 – Eliza Sophie Caird, English singer–songwriter
- April 19 – Haruna Kojima, Japanese singer, actress, and idol (AKB48)
- April 21
  - o Robbie Amell, Canadian actor
  - o Sophie Rundle, English actress
  - o Christoph Sanders, American actor
- April 25
  - o Sara Paxton, American actress
  - o Laura Lepistö, Finnish figure skater
  - o James Sheppard, Canadian ice hockey player
- April 26 – Gareth Evans, English footballer
- April 27 – Semyon Varlamov, Russian ice hockey player
- April 28 – Juan Mata, Spanish footballer
- April 29
  - o Alfred Hui, Hong Kong singer
  - o Jonathan Toews, Canadian hockey player
  - o Younha, Korean-born singer
- April 30 – Ana de Armas, Cuban actress

May

Adele

Nikki Reed

Gavin Free

- May 1
  - Anushka Sharma, Indian actress
  - Nicholas Braun, American actor
- May 4 – Kellie Loder, Canadian singer-songwriter
- May 5
  - Adele, English singer-songwriter
  - Brooke Hogan, American reality star and singer
  - Skye Sweetnam, Canadian singer
- May 6 – Ryan Anderson, American basketball player
- May 7 – Brandon Jones, American actor
- May 11
  - Ace Hood, American rapper
  - Brad Marchand, Canadian ice hockey player
- May 12
  - Marcelo Vieira, Brazilian footballer
  - Marky Cielo, Filipino actor and dancer (d. 2008)
- May 15 – Marcus Collins, English singer
- May 17
  - Nikki Reed, American actress
  - Jennison Myrie-Williams, English footballer
  - Freddie Hogan, British actor
- May 18
  - Ryan Cooley, Canadian actor
  - Taeyang, South Korean recording artist and model
- May 19 – Lily Cole, English supermodel
- May 21 – Park Gyu-ri, South Korean idol singer
- May 23
  - Gavin Free, English cinematographer
  - Morgan Pressel, American professional golfer
  - Tia Bajpai, Indian singer, television and film actress

- o Roope Ranta, Finnish professional ice hockey player
- o Danny de Jong, Dutch actor
- o Zachary "Kid Yamaka" Wohlman, American boxer
- May 24
  - o Billy Gilman, American singer
  - o Monica Lin Brown, U.S. Army medic, Silver Star recipient
- May 25
  - o Adrián González Morales, Spanish footballer
  - o Cameron van der Burgh, South African swimmer
- May 26
  - o Dani Samuels, Australian discus thrower
  - o Juan Cuadrado, Colombian footballer
  - o Joel Selwood, Australian rules footballer
- May 27 – Starshell, American actress, model, songwriter and singer
- May 28
  - o Cheng Fei, Chinese gymnast
  - o Percy Harvin, American football wide receiver
- May 29 – Tobin Heath, FIFA Women's World Cup silver medal winning soccer player for the United States
- May 31
  - o Hope Partlow, American pop singer
  - o Lisa Bund, German pop singer

June

Sergio Agüero

Michael Cera

Mae Whitman

Stephanie Rice

- June 1
    - Nami Tamaki, Japanese singer
    - Javier Hernández, Mexican footballer
- June 2 – Sergio Agüero, Argentine footballer
- June 4 – Li Man, Chinese actress
- June 5
    - Nuh Omar, Pakistani writer and director
    - Sam Slocombe, English footballer
- June 6 – Arianna Errigo, Italian fencer
- June 7
    - Michael Cera, Canadian actor
    - Ekaterina Makarova, Russian tennis player
    - Milan Lucic, Canadian professional ice hockey player
- June 8 – Reinaldo Zavarce, award-winning Venezuelan actor and singer
- June 9
    - Mae Whitman, American actress
    - Sokratis Papastathopoulos, Greek footballer
    - Lauren Landa, American voice actress

- June 11
  - Yui Aragaki, Japanese model, actress and singer
  - Claire Holt, Australian actress
- June 12
  - Eren Derdiyok, Swiss footballer
  - Cody Horn, American actress and model
- June 13 – Gabe Carimi, American football player
- June 14 – Kevin McHale, American actor, dancer and singer
- June 15 – Cristopher Toselli, Chilean footballer
- June 16 – Keshia Chanté, Canadian singer-songwriter, model and actress
- June 17 – Stephanie Rice, Australian swimmer
- June 21 – Alejandro Ramírez, Costa Rican chess Grandmaster
- June 22
  - Omri Casspi, Israeli basketball player
  - Portia Doubleday, American actress
  - Miliyah Kato, Japanese pop and urban singer-songwriter
- June 23
  - Isabella Leong, Hong Kong singer, actress and model
  - Chellsie Memmel, American gymnast
  - Jasmine Kara, Swedish singer and songwriter
- June 24
  - Micah Richards, English footballer
  - Nichkhun Horvejkul, Thai singer
  - Candice Patton, American actress
- June 25
  - Osama Ali, Iraqi footballer
  - Therese Johaug, Norwegian cross-country skier

- o Mark Haskins, English professional wrestler
- June 26
  - o Samanda (Amanda and Samantha Marchant), British acting duo
  - o Remy LaCroix, American pornographic actress
- June 27
  - o Alanna Masterson, American actress
  - o Matthew Špiranović, Australian footballer
- June 28 – Kanon Wakeshima, Japanese singer and cellist
- June 29 – Éver Banega, Argentine footballer
- June 30
  - o Pierdavide Carone, Italian singer-songwriter
  - o James Preston, American actor

July

Sayaka Akimoto

Colton Haynes

Julianne Hough

- July 2 – Lee Chung-yong, Korean footballer
- July 4 – Angelique Boyer, French-Mexican actress and singer
- July 7
  - Venus Raj, Filipina beauty queen and host
  - Natalie Mejia, American singer and songwriter
  - Jack Whitehall, English comedian
- July 8
  - Miki Roqué, Spanish footballer

- Rachael Finch, Australian beauty pageant titleholder and television reporter
- July 10
  - Manjari Phadnis, Indian film actress
  - Heather Hemmens, American actress
- July 11 – Joan Smalls, Puerto Rican model
- July 12 – LeSean McCoy, American football player
- July 13
  - He Pingping, Mongolian & Guinness World Records shortest man able to walk (d. 2010)
  - Steven R. McQueen, American actor
  - Colton Haynes, American actor and model
  - Tulisa Contostavlos, British singer-songwriter
- July 14 – James Vaughan, English footballer
- July 15 – Aimee Carrero, American actress
- July 16 – Sergio Busquets, Spanish footballer
- July 17 – Summer Bishil, American actress
- July 18 – Ambyr Childers, American actress
- July 19
  - Shane Dawson, American YouTube comedian and actor
  - Cherami Leigh, American actress and voice actress
- July 20
  - Julianne Hough, American ballroom dancer, country music singer and actress
  - Stephen Strasburg, American baseball player
- July 21 – DeAndre Jordan, American basketball player
- July 23 – Paul Anderson, English footballer
- July 24 – Han Seung-yeon, South Korean idol singer dancer and actress
- July 25

- Linsey Godfrey, American actress
- Anthony Stokes, Irish footballer
- Heather Marks, Canadian model
- Sarah Geronimo, Filipina singer and actress
- July 26
  - Sayaka Akimoto, Japanese singer, actress and idol (AKB48)
  - Francia Raisa, American actress
- July 28
  - Ayla Brown, American recording artist and former NCAA basketball player
  - Gunnar Nelson (fighter), Icelandic mixed martial artist and Brazilian jiu-jitsu practitioner
- July 30 – Alexander Vlahos, Welsh actor
- July 31
  - Krystal Meyers, American singer/songwriter/musician
  - Charlie Carver, American actor

August

Rupert Grint

Alexa Vega

Rumer Willis

Tara Teng

Veronica Roth

- August 1
  - Max Carver, American actor
  - Sasha Jackson, British actress
- August 2
  - Nayer, American pop singer
  - Golden Tate, American football player
- August 4 – Jen Lilley, American actress
- August 5
  - Eddie Nolan, Irish footballer
  - Federica Pellegrini, Italian swimmer
  - Kendra Spears, American model
- August 7 – Beanie Wells, American football running back
- August 8
  - Princess Beatrice of York, British princess and daughter of Prince Andrew, Duke of York and Sarah, Duchess of York
  - Mădălina Diana Ghenea, Romanian-born actress and model
- August 12
  - Leah Pipes, American actress
  - Justin Gaston, American singer-songwriter, model and actor

- August 13 – MØ, Danish singer
- August 15- Zaira Nara, Argentine model
- August 16
  - Ismaïl Aissati, Moroccan footballer
  - Tara Teng, Canadian model, human rights activist, blogger, public speaker and television presenter
  - Rumer Willis, American actress and singer
- August 17
  - Erika Toda, Japanese actress
  - Jihadi John, Kuwaiti member of ISIS (d. 2015)
- August 18
  - G-Dragon, Korean bandleader (Big Bang)
  - Jack Hobbs, English footballer
  - Travis Tedford, American actor
- August 19
  - Hoodie Allen, American hip-hop artist
  - Veronica Roth, American novelist and short story writer
- August 21
  - Kacey Musgraves, American country music artist
  - Robert Lewandowski, Polish footballer
- August 22
  - Mitchell Langerak, Australian football player
  - Dávid Verrasztó, Hungarian swimmer
- August 23
  - Kimberly Matula, American actress
  - Jeremy Lin, American basketball player
  - Alice Glass, Canadian singer
- August 24 – Rupert Grint, English actor
- August 25

- o Alexandra Burke, English singer
  - o Ray Quinn, English actor, singer, and dancer
- August 26
  - o Tori Black, American pornographic actress
  - o Evan Ross, American actor and musician
  - o Erik Hassle, Swedish pop singer-songwriter
- August 27 – Alexa Vega, American actress
- August 29 – Bartosz Kurek, Polish volleyball player
- August 30 – Ernests Gulbis, Latvian tennis player
- August 31 – Tanaya Henry, American model and actress

September

Jérôme Boateng

Chelsea Kane

Kevin Durant

- September 1
  - Simona de Silvestro, Swiss race car drive
  - Mushfiqur Rahim, Bangladeshi cricketer
- September 2
  - Ishant Sharma, Indian cricketer
  - Javi Martínez, Spanish footballer
- September 3 – Jérôme Boateng, German footballer
- September 5
  - Nuri Şahin, Turkish footballer
  - Felipe Caicedo, Ecuadorian association footballer
- September 6
  - Sargun Mehta, Indian model, comedian, dancer, presenter and actress.
  - Max George, British singer
- September 7
  - Kevin Love, American basketball player
  - Paul Iacono, American actor
- September 8 – Chantal Jones, American fashion model and actress
- September 9
  - McKey Sullivan, American fashion model
  - JM de Guzman, Filipino actor

- September 10
  - Jordan Staal, Canadian hockey player
  - Coco Rocha, Canadian fashion model
  - Jared Lee Loughner, American perpetrator/gunman of the 2011 Tucson shooting
- September 11 – Lee Yong-dae, South Korean male badminton player
- September 12
  - Prachi Desai, Indian film and television actress
  - Amanda Jenssen, Swedish singer
  - Matt Martians, American record producer
- September 13 – John Park, American singer
- September 14 – Martin Fourcade, French biathlete
- September 15
  - Chelsea Kane, American actress and singer
  - Nuno Roque, Portuguese actor
- September 16 – Teddy Geiger, American singer-songwriter
- September 17 – Pavel Mamayev, Russian footballer
- September 18
  - Arizona Muse, American model
  - Lukas Graham, Danish singer
- September 19
  - Katrina Bowden, American actress
- September 21
  - Doug Baldwin, American football player
  - Bilawal Bhutto Zardari, Chairman of the Pakistan Peoples Party
- September 22 – Bethany Dillon, contemporary Christian music artist

- September 23 – Juan Martín del Potro, Argentine tennis player
- September 25 – Ragasya, Indian actress and model
- September 26
  - Kiira Korpi, Finnish figure skater
  - Sandhya, Indian film actress
  - James Blake, English electronic music producer and singer-songwriter
- September 28
  - Esmée Denters, Dutch singer
  - Bill Sweatt, American ice hockey left winger
- September 29
  - Kevin Durant, American basketball player
  - Justin Nozuka, American-Canadian singer-songwriter

October

Cariba Heine

Alicia Vikander

Melissa Benoist

Janel Parrish

- October 1 – Cariba Heine, Australian actress and performer

- October 2 – Andreas Moe, Swedish singer-songwriter, producer, and multi-instrumentalist
- October 3
  - ASAP Rocky, American rapper and music video director
  - Alicia Vikander, Swedish actress
- October 4
  - Ashley Banjo, British choreographer (Diversity)
  - Melissa Benoist, American actress and singer
  - Derrick Rose, American basketball player
- October 5
  - Bahar Kızıl, German singer-songwriter
  - Maja Salvador, Filipina actress
- October 6 – Maki Horikita, Japanese actress
- October 7 – Diego Costa, Spanish footballer
- October 8 – Hanne Gaby Odiele, Belgian model
- October 11 – Rika Izumi, Japanese actress
- October 14
  - Max Thieriot, American actor
  - Pia Toscano, American singer; American Idol contestant
- October 15 – Mesut Özil, German football player
- October 17 – Yuko Oshima, Japanese idol, singer and actress (AKB48)
- October 20
  - Risa Niigaki, Japanese singer
  - Candice Swanepoel, South African supermodel
- October 21 – Blanca Suárez, Spanish actress
- October 22 – Parineeti Chopra, Bollywood actress.
- October 27 – Evan Turner, American basketball player

- October 28
    - ASAP Ferg, American hip hop musician
    - Edd Gould, British flash animator, creator of Eddsworld (d. 2012)
    - Devon Murray, Irish actor
- October 30 – Janel Parrish, American actress and singer-songwriter
- October 31 – Sébastien Buemi, Swiss racing driver

November

Emma Stone

Conchita Wurst

Jamie Campbell Bower

Phillip Hughes

- November 1
    - Ai Fukuhara, Japanese table tennis player
    - Scott Arfield, Scottish footballer
- November 2
    - Elgiazar Farashyan, Belarusian singer (3+2)
    - Julia Görges, German professional tennis player
- November 3 – Angus McLaren, Australian actor
- November 5 – Virat Kohli, Indian international cricketer
- November 6
    - Emma Stone, American actress
    - Conchita Wurst, Austrian singer, Eurovision Song Contest 2014 winner

- November 7
  - Alexandr Dolgopolov, Ukrainian tennis player
  - Elsa Hosk, Swedish model
  - Tinie Tempah, English rapper
- November 8
  - Jessica Lowndes, Canadian actress and singer
  - Jared Kusnitz, American film and television actor
- November 9
  - Nikki Blonsky, American actress and singer
  - Analeigh Tipton, American figure skater and actress
- November 12 – Russell Westbrook, American basketball player
- November 15 – B.o.B, American rapper, singer and record producer
- November 19 – Patrick Kane, American hockey player
- November 20 – Rhys Wakefield, Australian actor
- November 21 – Len Väljas, Canadian cross-country skier
- November 22 – Jamie Campbell Bower, English actor
- November 24 – Sabi, American pop singer-songwriter, dancer and actress
- November 25
  - Jay Spearing, English footballer
  - Nodar Kumaritashvili, Georgian lugar (d. 2010)
- November 29 – Russell Wilson, American football player
- November 30
  - Phillip Hughes, Australian cricketer (d. 2014)
  - Eir Aoi, Japanese singer
  - Rotimi, singer-songwriter, actor, and model

December

Zoe Kravitz

Emily Browning

Vanessa Hudgens

Hayley Williams

- December 1 – Zoë Kravitz, American actress
- December 2
  - Alfred Enoch, British actor
  - Athena, Filipina singer, stage actress
- December 4
  - Mario Maurer, Thai model and actor
  - Yeng Constantino, Filipina singer
- December 5 – Miralem Sulejmani, Serbian football player
- December 6 – Sandra Nurmsalu, Estonian musician
- December 7 – Emily Browning, Australian actress
- December 12
  - Ashley Hinshaw, American actress and model
  - Hahm Eun-jung, South Korean singer
- December 13 – Oliver Lancashire, English footballer
- December 14
  - Nicolas Batum, French basketball player
  - Nate Ebner, American football player
  - Vanessa Hudgens, American actress and singer
- December 16
  - Anna Popplewell, English actress
  - Mats Hummels, German footballer
- December 17 – David Rudisha, Kenyan middle-distance runner
- December 19 – Alexis Sánchez, Chilean footballer
- December 23
  - Eri Kamei, Japanese singer
  - Mallory Hagan, American beauty pageant titleholder
- December 25
  - Eric Gordon, American basketball player
  - Marco Mengoni, Italian singer-songwriter

- December 27 – Hayley Williams, American singer (Paramore)
- December 28
  - Ched Evans, Welsh footballer
  - Florrie, English pop singer
- December 29
  - Ágnes Szávay, Hungarian tennis player
  - Michaela Kocianova, Slovak model
- December 30
  - Kirsty-Leigh Porter, English actress
  - Leon Jackson, Scottish singer
  - Jena Sims, American beauty queen

Date unknown

- Benjamin Fodor alias Phoenix Jones, American superhero/vigilante
- Ricky Norwood, English actor

Deaths

January

Georgy Malenkov

- January 1 – Margot Bryant, British actress (b. 1897)
- January 2 – E. B. Ford, British geneticist (b. 1901)
- January 5 – Pete Maravich, American basketball player (b. 1947)
- January 6 – L. P. Davies, English novelist (b. 1914)
- January 7 – Trevor Howard, British actor (b. 1913)
- January 11 – Gregory "Pappy" Boyington, American pilot, United States Marine Corps fighter ace (b. 1912)
- January 12 – Hiram Bingham IV, American diplomat (b. 1903)
- January 13 – Chiang Ching-kuo, Chinese politician, 3rd President of the Republic of China (b. 1910)
- January 14 – Georgy Malenkov, Soviet politician, 5th Prime Minister of the Soviet Union (b. 1902)
- January 15 – Seán MacBride, Irish Republican Army leader, recipient of the Nobel Peace Prize (b. 1904)
- January 16 – Ballard Berkeley, British actor (b. 1904)
- January 20 – Philippe de Rothschild, French vineyard owner (b. 1902)
- January 21 – Vincent Lingiari, Australian Aboriginal rights activist (b. 1908)
- January 22 – Parker Fennelly, American comedian and actor (b. 1891)
- January 25 – Colleen Moore, American actress (b. 1899)
- January 28 – Klaus Fuchs, German-British physicist and spy (b. 1911)

February

Kurt Mahler

Richard Feynman

- February 1 – Heather O'Rourke, American actress (b. 1975)
- February 3 – Robert Duncan, American poet (b. 1919)
- February 5 – Emeric Pressburger, Hungarian-British film producer (b. 1902)
- February 11 – Marion Crawford, Scottish nanny of Elizabeth II (b. 1909)
- February 12 – S. Nadarajah, Sri Lankan Tamil lawyer and politician
- February 13

- o Ron Embleton, British comics artist and illustrator (b. 1930)
- o Léon Goossens. British oboist (b. 1897)
- February 14 – Frederick Loewe, Austrian-American composer (b. 1901)
- February 15 – Richard Feynman, American physicist, Nobel Prize laureate (b. 1918)
- February 16 – Karp Osipovich Lykov, Russian Old Believer and survivalist
- February 19
  - o René Char, French poet (b. 1907)
  - o André Frédéric Cournand, French-American physician, recipient of the Nobel Prize in Physiology or Medicine (b. 1895)
- February 25 – Kurt Mahler, German-Australian mathematician (b. 1903)

March

Kurt Georg Kiesinger

- March 1 – Joe Besser, American actor and comedian (b. 1907)
- March 3 – Lois Wilson, American actress (b. 1894)

- March 5 – Alberto Olmedo, Argentine comedian and actor (b. 1933)
- March 7
  - Divine, American singer and actor (b. 1945)
  - Edmund Berkeley, American scientist (b. 1909)
  - Robert Livingston, American actor (b. 1904)
- March 8
  - Werner Hartmann, German physicist (b. 1912)
  - Henryk Szeryng, Polish-born violinist (b. 1918)
- March 9 – Kurt Georg Kiesinger, German politician, 3rd Chancellor of Germany (b. 1904)
- March 10
  - Glenn Cunningham, American Olympic athlete (b. 1909)
  - Andy Gibb, British singer (b. 1958)
  - Phạm Hùng, Vietnamese prime minister (b. 1912)
- March 13
  - Olive Carey, American actress (b. 1896)
  - John Holmes, American pornographic actor (b. 1944)
- March 16 – Erich Probst, Austrian football player (b. 1927)
- March 20
  - Gil Evans, American jazz pianist (b. 1912)
  - Ralph Wright, Writer and American actor (b. 1908)
- March 21 – Edd Roush, American baseball player (Cincinnati Reds) and member of the MLB Hall of Fame, (b. 1893)
- March 22 – Lester Rawlins, American stage and screen director (b. 1924)
- March 25 – Robert Joffrey, American dancer and choreographer (b. 1930)

- March 31 – Sir William McMahon, twentieth Prime Minister of Australia (b. 1908)

April

Alan Paton

- April 1 – Jim Jordan, American actor (b. 1896)
- April 3 – Milton Caniff, American cartoonist (b. 1907)
- April 6 – John Clements, British actor (b. 1910)
- April 11
  - Hermann Graf, German fighter ace (b. 1912)
  - Jesse L. Lasky, Jr., American screenwriter (b. 1910)
- April 12
  - Harry McShane, Scottish socialist (b. 1891)
  - Alan Paton, South African author (b. 1903)
- April 15 – Kenneth Williams, British actor and raconteur (b. 1926)
- April 17
  - Louise Nevelson, Ukrainian-American sculptor (b. 1900)
  - Eva Novak, American actress (b. 1898)
- April 18 – Pierre Desproges, French humorist (b. 1939)

- April 21 – I. A. L. Diamond, American screenwriter (b. 1920)
- April 22 – Irene Rich, American actress (b. 1891)
- April 23 – Michael Ramsey, British bishop, 100th Archbishop of Canterbury (b. 1904)
- April 26
  - James McCracken, American tenor (b. 1926)
  - Valerie Solanas, American author (b. 1936)
- April 27 – David Scarboro, British actor (b. 1968)

May

Robert A. Heinlein

Willem Drees

Ella Raines

- May 3 – Lev Pontryagin, Russian mathematician (b. 1908)
- May 5 – George Rose, English actor (b. 1920)
- May 8 – Robert A. Heinlein, American science fiction author (b. 1907)
- May 10
  - Shen Congwen, Chinese writer (b. 1902)
  - Ciarán Bourke, Irish musician (b. 1935)
- May 11 – Kim Philby, British spy (b. 1912)
- May 12 – Chet Baker, American jazz trumpeter (b. 1929)
- May 14 – Willem Drees, Dutch politician and historian, Prime Minister of the Netherlands (1948–1958) (b. 1886)
- May 15
  - Andrew Duggan, American actor (b. 1923)
  - Greta Nissen, Norwegian-born actress (b. 1905)
- May 16 – Charles Keeping, British illustrator (b. 1924)
- May 18 – Daws Butler, voice actor (b. 1916)
- May 21 – Sammy Davis Sr., American dancer (b. 1900)
- May 23 – Aya Kitō, Japanese Writer (b. 1962)
- May 25 – Ernst Ruska, German physicist, Nobel Prize laureate (b. 1906)
- May 27 – Florida Friebus, American actor (b. 1909)
- May 29 – Vladimír Menšík, Czech actor (b. 1929)

- May 30 – Ella Raines, American actress (b. 1920)
- May 31 – Arthur Olliver, Australian footballer (b. 1916)

June

Giuseppe Saragat

- June 2 – Raj Kapoor, Indian actor, producer and director (b. 1924)
- June 8 – Eli Mintz, American actor (b. 1904)
- June 10 – Louis L'Amour, American writer (b. 1908)
- June 11 – Giuseppe Saragat, former President of Italy (b. 1898)
- June 16 – Kim Milford, American actor and singer (b. 1951)
- June 18 – Wilford Leach, American theater director (b. 1929)
- June 22 – Dennis Day, Irish-American singer and radio and television personality (b. 1916)
- June 25 – Hillel Slovak, Israeli-American guitarist (Red Hot Chili Peppers) (b. 1962)

July

- July 3 – Gabriel Dell, American actor (b. 1919)

- July 4 – Adrian Adonis, American wrestler (b. 1954)
- July 8 – Ray Barbuti, American athlete (b. 1905)
- July 12 – Joshua Logan, American stage and film director (b. 1908)
- July 17 – Bruiser Brody, American professional wrestler (b. 1946)
- July 18 – Nico, singer-songwriter, fashion model, actress and Warhol socialite (b. 1938)
- July 21 – Jack Clark, American television personality and game show host (b. 1921)
- July 25
  - Douglas Hickox, English film director (b. 1929)
  - Judith Barsi, American child actress and murder victim (b. 1978)
- July 27 – Frank Zamboni, American inventor (b. 1901)
- July 31 – Trinidad Silva, American actor (b. 1950)

August

Enzo Ferrari

- August 1 – Florence Eldridge, American actress (b. 1901)

- August 2 – Raymond Carver, American short-story writer and poet (b. 1938)
- August 5
  - Colin Higgins, American film director (b. 1941)
  - Ralph Meeker, American actor (b. 1920)
- August 8
  - Félix Leclerc, French-Canadian poet and singer (b. 1914)
  - Alan Napier, English actor (b. 1903)
- August 9
  - Giacinto Scelsi, Italian composer (b. 1905)
  - Ramón Valdés, Mexican actor (b. 1923)
- August 10
  - Arnulfo Arias, three-term President of Panama (b. 1901)
  - Adela Rogers St. Johns, American journalist and screenwriter (b. 1893)
- August 11 – Anne Ramsey, American actress (b. 1929)
- August 12 – Jean-Michel Basquiat, American musician/graffiti painter (b. 1960)
- August 14
  - Robert Calvert, writer, poet, and musician (b. 1944)
  - Enzo Ferrari, Italian car maker (b. 1898)
- August 17
  - Franklin Delano Roosevelt, Jr., American lawyer and politician (b. 1914)
  - Muhammad Zia-ul-Haq, leader of Pakistan (b. 1924)
- August 21 – Ray Eames, American artist, designer, and filmmaker (b. 1912)
- August 24 – Leonard Frey, American actor (b. 1938)
- August 27

- o William Sargant, British psychiatrist (b. 1907)
- o Kerry Lloyd, American role-playing game designer (b. 1941)
- o Mario Montenegro, Filipino actor (b. 1928)
- August 28
  - o Hazel Dawn, American actress (b. 1891)
  - o Max Shulman, American comedic writer (b. 1919)
- August 29 – David A. Hargrave, American role-playing game designer (b. 1946)

September

Luis Walter Alvarez

- September 1 – Luis Walter Alvarez, American physicist, Nobel Prize laureate (b. 1911)
- September 5 – Gert Fröbe, German actor (b. 1913)
- September 6 – Harold Rosson, American cinematographer (b. 1895)
- September 11 – John Sylvester White, American actor (b. 1919)
- September 12 – Roger Hargreaves, English author (b. 1935)
- September 16 – Dick Pym, English footballer (b. 1893)

- September 18
  - Mohammad-Hossein Shahriar, Iranian Azari poet (b. 1906)
  - Alan Watt (diplomat), Australian public servant (b. 1901)
- September 20 – Roy Kinnear, British actor (b. 1934)
- September 21
  - Glenn Robert Davis American politician (b. 1914)
  - Henry Koster, German-born film director (b. 1905)
- September 28
  - Charles Addams, American cartoonist (b. 1912)
  - Ethel Grandin, American actress (b. 1894)
- September 30 – Trường Chinh, former President of Vietnam (b. 1907)

October

John Houseman

- October 1
  - Lucien Ballard, American cinematographer (b. 1908)
  - Sacheverell Sitwell, English writer (b. 1897)
  - Pavle Vuisić, Yugoslav actor (b. 1926)

- October 2 – Alec Issigonis, Greek-British engineer (b. 1906)
- October 3 – Franz Josef Strauss, German politician (b. 1915)
- October 7 – Billy Daniels, American singer (b. 1915)
- October 9 –
  - Jackie Milburn, English footballer (b. 1924)
  - Felix Wankel, German mechanical engineer (b. 1902)
- October 11
  - Wayland Flowers, American puppeteer (b. 1939)
  - Bonita Granville, American actress (b. 1923)
- October 12
  - Ken Murray, American actor (b. 1903)
  - Ruth Manning-Sanders, British children's author (b. 1895)
- October 13 – Melvin Frank, American screenwriter and director (b. 1913)
- October 15 – Kaikhosru Shapurji Sorabji, English composer, music critic, pianist, and writer (b. 1892)
- October 18 – Frederick Ashton, English dancer and choreographer (b. 1904)
- October 19 – Son House, American musician (b. 1902)
- October 22 – Henry Armstrong, American boxer (b. 1912)
- October 23 – Asashio Tarō III, Sumo wrestler (b. 1929)
- October 27 – Charles Hawtrey, English actor (b. 1914)
- October 31 – John Houseman, Romanian-American actor and producer (b. 1902)

November

John Carradine

- November 1 – George J. Folsey, American cinematographer (b. 1898)
- November 7
  - Bill Hoest, American cartoonist (b. 1926)
  - Sy Mah, Canadian marathoner (b. 1926)
- November 9
  - David Bauer, Canadian ice hockey player (b. 1924)
  - Clarke Hinkle, American football player (Green Bay Packers) and member of the Pro Football Hall of Fame (b. 1909)
  - John N. Mitchell, American lawyer, 67th United States Attorney General (b. 1913)
  - Rosemary Timperley, British author (b. 1920)
- November 11 – William Ifor Jones, Welsh conductor and organist (b. 1900)
- November 12
  - Vet Boswell, American singer (b. 1911)
  - Lyman Lemnitzer, American Army General (b. 1899)
- November 13 – Antal Doráti, Hungarian conductor (b. 1906)
- November 14 – Takeo Miki, Japanese politician, 41st Prime Minister of Japan (b. 1909)

- November 15 – Mona Washbourne, British actress (b. 1903)
- November 17 – Sheilah Graham, English-born gossip columnist (b. 1904)
- November 19 – Christina Onassis, American shipping magnate (b. 1950)
- November 21 – Carl Hubbell, American baseball player (New York Giants) and member of the MLB Hall of Fame (b. 1903)
- November 22
  - Luis Barragán, Mexican architect (b. 1902)
  - Raymond Dart, Australian anatomist and anthropologist (b. 1893)
- November 27 – John Carradine, American actor (b. 1906)
- November 29 – Donald Keyhoe, American ufologist (b. 1897)

December

Roy Orbison

Nikolaas Tinbergen

- December 2 – Tata Giacobetti, Italian singer and lyricist (Quartetto Cetra) (b. 1922)
- December 4 – Osman Achmatowicz, Polish chemist (b. 1899)
- December 6
  - Roy Orbison, American singer (b. 1936)
  - Timothy Patrick Murphy, American actor (b. 1959)
- December 10 – Richard S. Castellano, American actor (b. 1933)
- December 13 – Roy Urquhart, British general (b. 1901)
- December 16 – Sylvester James, American R&B singer, disco performer (b. 1948)
- December 17 – Jerry Hopper, American film and television director (b. 1907)
- December 20 – Max Robinson, American broadcast journalist, and ABC News *World News Tonight* co-anchor (b. 1939)
- December 21
  - Bob Steele, American actor (b. 1907)
  - Nikolaas Tinbergen, Dutch ornithologist, recipient of the Nobel Prize in Physiology or Medicine (b. 1907)

- December 22 – Francisco Alves Mendes Filho, Brazilian environmental activist (murdered) (b. 1944)
- December 23 – Carlo Scorza, Italian Fascist politician (b. 1897)
- December 26
  - John Loder, English actor (b. 1898)
  - Glenn McCarthy, American oil tycoon and businessman (b. 1907)
  - Pablo Sorozábal, Basque-Spanish composer (b. 1897)
- December 27
  - Hal Ashby, American film director (b. 1929)
  - Jess Oppenheimer, American radio and television producer (b. 1913)
- December 30 – Isamu Noguchi, Japanese-American artist (b. 1904)

Nobel Prizes

- Physics – Leon M. Lederman, Melvin Schwartz, Jack Steinberger
- Chemistry – Johann Deisenhofer, Robert Huber, Hartmut Michel
- Medicine – Sir James W. Black, Gertrude B. Elion, George H. Hitchings
- Literature – Naguib Mahfouz
- Peace – The United Nations Peace-Keeping Forces.
- The Bank of Sweden Prize in Economic Sciences in Memory of Alfred Nobel – Maurice Allais

In the News.

The Hubble Space Telescope Goes into operation to explore deep space and is still in full use today.

After 8 years and 1.5 million dead the Iran -- Iraq war ends.

Suspected Libyan terrorist bomb explodes on Pan Am jet over Lockerbie in Scotland on December 21st killing all 259 on board.

Australia celebrates its bicentennial.

The **English Pound** Note ceases to be legal Tender.

Ben Johnson wins the 100m gold at the Seoul Olympics and is then disqualified for taking the anabolic steroid, Stanozol.

Salmonella is found in Eggs in Britain causing problems for British Farmers.

The Summer Olympics are held in Seoul, South Korea.

US Space Shuttle program resumes 2 1/2 years after Challenger disaster.

Prince Charles escapes avalanche in Switzerland.

The **US** Stealth Bomber is unveiled.

Popular Films - Rain Man, Who Framed Roger Rabbit, Big, Twins, Crocodile Dundee II, Die Hard.

1988 Calendar.

January 1988
Sun	Mon	Tue	Wed	Thu	Fri	Sat
					1	2
3	4	5	6	7	8	9
10	11	12	13	14	15	16
17	18	19	20	21	22	23
24	25	26	27	28	29	30
31						

February 1988
Sun	Mon	Tue	Wed	Thu	Fri	Sat
	1	2	3	4	5	6
7	8	9	10	11	12	13
14	15	16	17	18	19	20
21	22	23	24	25	26	27
28	29					

March 1988
Sun	Mon	Tue	Wed	Thu	Fri	Sat
		1	2	3	4	5
6	7	8	9	10	11	12
13	14	15	16	17	18	19
20	21	22	23	24	25	26
27	28	29	30	31		

April 1988
Sun	Mon	Tue	Wed	Thu	Fri	Sat
					1	2
3	4	5	6	7	8	9
10	11	12	13	14	15	16
17	18	19	20	21	22	23
24	25	26	27	28	29	30

May 1988
Sun	Mon	Tue	Wed	Thu	Fri	Sat
1	2	3	4	5	6	7
8	9	10	11	12	13	14
15	16	17	18	19	20	21
22	23	24	25	26	27	28
29	30	31				

June 1988
Sun	Mon	Tue	Wed	Thu	Fri	Sat
			1	2	3	4
5	6	7	8	9	10	11
12	13	14	15	16	17	18
19	20	21	22	23	24	25
26	27	28	29	30		

July 1988
Sun	Mon	Tue	Wed	Thu	Fri	Sat
					1	2
3	4	5	6	7	8	9
10	11	12	13	14	15	16
17	18	19	20	21	22	23
24	25	26	27	28	29	30
31						

August 1988
Sun	Mon	Tue	Wed	Thu	Fri	Sat
	1	2	3	4	5	6
7	8	9	10	11	12	13
14	15	16	17	18	19	20
21	22	23	24	25	26	27
28	29	30	31			

September 1988
Sun	Mon	Tue	Wed	Thu	Fri	Sat
				1	2	3
4	5	6	7	8	9	10
11	12	13	14	15	16	17
18	19	20	21	22	23	24
25	26	27	28	29	30	

October 1988
Sun	Mon	Tue	Wed	Thu	Fri	Sat
						1
2	3	4	5	6	7	8
9	10	11	12	13	14	15
16	17	18	19	20	21	22
23	24	25	26	27	28	29
30	31					

November 1988
Sun	Mon	Tue	Wed	Thu	Fri	Sat
		1	2	3	4	5
6	7	8	9	10	11	12
13	14	15	16	17	18	19
20	21	22	23	24	25	26
27	28	29	30			

December 1988
Sun	Mon	Tue	Wed	Thu	Fri	Sat
				1	2	3
4	5	6	7	8	9	10
11	12	13	14	15	16	17
18	19	20	21	22	23	24
25	26	27	28	29	30	31

www.thepeoplehistory.com

www.ingramcontent.com/pod-product-compliance
Lightning Source LLC
Chambersburg PA
CBHW071223280526
45787CB00002B/785